THE BAD GUYS

EPISODE 5   EPISODE 6

■SCHOLASTIC

Scholastic Children's Books
An imprint of Scholastic Ltd
Euston House, 24 Eversholt Street, London, NW1 1DB, UK
Registered office: Westfield Road, Southam, Warwickshire, CV47 0RA
SCHOLASTIC and associated logos are trademarks and/or
registered trademarks of Scholastic Inc.

Bad Guys Episode 5 first published in Australia by Scholastic
Australia, 2017
First published in the UK by Scholastic Ltd, 2018

Bad Guys Episode 6 first published in Australia by Scholastic
Australia, 2017
First published in the UK by Scholastic Ltd, 2018

This edition first published 2018

Copyright © Aaron Blabey, 2017

The right of Aaron Blabey to be identified as the author and illustrator of this
work has been asserted by him.

ISBN 978 1407 19207 9

A CIP catalogue record for this book
is available from the British Library.

Printed by CPI Group (UK) Ltd, Croydon, CR0 4YY
Papers used by Scholastic Children's Books are made
from wood grown in sustainable forests.

5 7 9 10 8 6

www.scholastic.co.uk

AARON BLABEY

THE BAD GUYS

EPISODE 5 INTERGALACTIC GAS

Are we rolling? OK.

This is **TIFFANY FLUFFIT**
for 6 News.
Our television station has been
destroyed but we will keep
broadcasting as long as we can.

This is what we know . . .

Tiffany Fluffit
6 NEWS

Well, the flesh-eating zombie kittens were bad,

but they were **NOTHING** compared to this . . .

The world has been **OVERRUN** by zombie puppies,

zombie ponies, zombie dolphins, zombie bunnies

and, yes—**MORE** zombie kittens!

We believe this to be the work of the **EVIL**

DR RUPERT MARMALADE

but he has **COMPLETELY**

DISAPPEARED!

MARMALADE

There seems to be **NO WAY** to stop this.

It truly is

THE END OF THE WORLD!

In further news, those *other* monsters who recently caused trouble at the **CITY DOG POUND** and **SUNNYSIDE CHICKEN FARM** have tried to convince the authorities that they **KNOW** where Dr Marmalade is hiding.

Just have a look at this . . .

Officer! Please listen!

I think I speak for all of us when I say—

LISTEN UP, WOLF!

THE WORLD IS ENDING AND WE NEED

HEROES!

WHAT WE **DON'T** NEED IS A BUNCH

OF **STINKY,**

LYING . . .

· CHAPTER 1 ·
FLY ME TO THE MOON

I don't believe this!
What do you do when you are the
only ones who know the truth . . .

. . . BUT
NO-ONE
WILL
BELIEVE
YOU?!

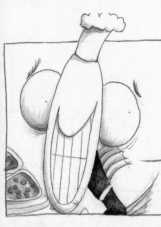

I'm keeping our spirits up, hermano, with succulent pockets of meat and beans.

They're good, too. I've had **SIX** already.

How can you eat when the world is ending?

I eat for comfort! It makes me feel safe!

DON'T JUDGE ME!

Thanks, Piranha.

No sweat, chico.

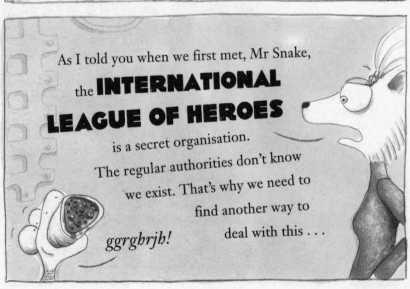

As I told you when we first met, Mr Snake,

the **INTERNATIONAL LEAGUE OF HEROES** is a secret organisation.
The regular authorities don't know we exist. That's why we need to find another way to deal with this . . .

ggrghrjh!

What do you suggest?

We need to . . .
borrow a rocket and
**GET TO
THE MOON
OURSELVES**.

Borrow?

She means **STEAL.**

WHAT?! Oh noooo, no, no, **NO!**
That's NOT part of the plan. No-one will EVER
believe we're **HEROES**
if we **STEAL** something.
Especially a rocket!
I mean, someone will
NOTICE if we **TAKE**
A WHOLE
SPACESHIP!
I won't
do it.

Mr Wolf, listen very carefully.

The world IS about to end.

The **ONLY** way to stop it is to get

to the moon. And **WE** are the only

ones who know the truth.

If we don't . . .

borrow a spaceship and destroy

the Cute-Zilla Ray . . .

. . . EVERYONE
ON THE FACE
OF THE EARTH
WILL DIE.

PERIOD.

Well, if you put it like that . . .

But will we bring it back?

If we survive this mission and
SAVE THE EARTH,
I'm pretty sure they'll let us keep it.
But yes, we will try our hardest to
bring it back . . .

In one piece?

Um . . . sure.

OK, I guess that's cool.

So, we need to find a spaceship, come up with a plan to get inside it, and then you'll fly us to the moon?

Well, yes. Except that last part. *I* don't know how to operate a spacecraft . . .

WHAT?!

But if you can't fly a rocket, how is this stupid plan meant to work?

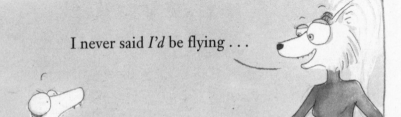

I never said *I'd* be flying . . .

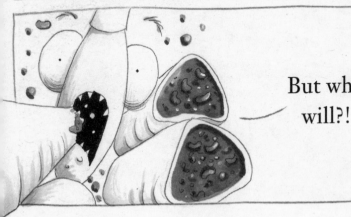

But who will?!

· CHAPTER 2 ·
WE HAVE
LIFT-OFF

Are you sure about this, Agent Fox?

Just do what I do, Mr Wolf, and we'll be fine . . .

HEY! You two! Where are you going with that . . .

. . . rocket?

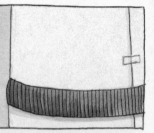

Sir! We have orders to get this booster rocket onto that spaceship! The world's gone crazy, huh?

That's pretty small for a booster rocket . . .

Yes, it is. But this little beauty is **FULL** of surprises.

As you were . . .

Wow. That was amazing! How did you *do* that?!

It's all about **CONFIDENCE,** Mr Wolf. You just need to believe you can do it, and everyone else will believe it too.

Yeah, yeah, I'd LOVE to hear more of this thrilling motivational speech, but can you PLEASE JUST GET US OUT OF HERE?!

OK, Snake.
Wait a minute . . .

You might want to look away for this bit . . .

You think **THAT'S** nasty?!
You weren't trapped *inside a shark*
with a tarantula **AND** an idiot
piranha carrying a **STINKY
BAG OF BURRITOS!**

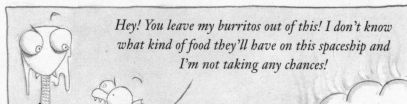

*Hey! You leave my burritos out of this! I don't know
what kind of food they'll have on this spaceship and
I'm not taking any chances!*

Geez! How many
did you bring?!

ENOUGH!
That's all you need to know!
I'VE GOT ENOUGH!

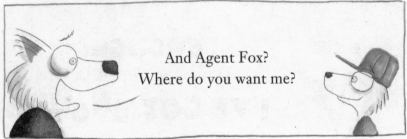

That's not for me
to say, Mr Wolf.
This is **YOUR** mission.

What?

Do you mean . . .
YOU'RE NOT
COMING?!

Someone has to
stay here and fight
the zombies . . .
and that means us –

**NO!** We can't do this without you! We're not **HALF** the heroes you are!

You're more like us than you know!

In fact, we used to be **JUST LIKE YOU**.

Maybe I'll tell you about it some day.

But right now, you have to go and save the world.

WE'RE COUNTING ON YOU.

We won't be able to hold back the zombies for long . . .

*Wolfie!* Hurry! We have to get out of here **RIGHT NOW!**

I'm proud of you, Mr Wolf.
Good luck!

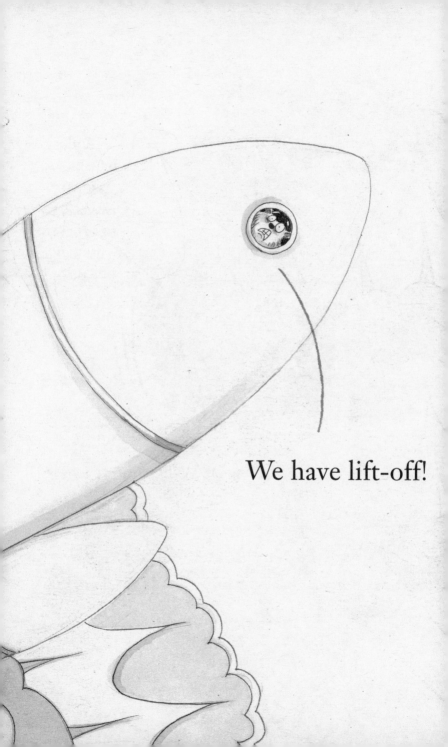

We have lift-off!

· CHAPTER 3 ·
ZERO GRAVITY, ZERO JEALOUSY?

And there goes the
final booster . . .

SPLAT!

Yo, chico!
My burrito bag burst.
Grab that, will you?

This is serious, Piranha!

How many of these have
you eaten, anyway?!

I'd rather
not say . . .

Don't give him a hard time, just because you're scared, Wolf.

I'm sorry! I just didn't think being a hero would be quite this stressful . . .

WHATEVER!

YOU keep getting us into these situations, so **DEAL WITH IT!**
If we survive, your precious Agent Fox will give you a **KISS.**
And if we don't . . .
well, it won't matter, will it?

You know what, Snake?

What?

Every time you talk about Agent Fox, you sound **JEALOUS.**

WHAT?! You think I'm jealous that Agent Fox thinks this numbskull is 'sweet'?

Nope.

I think you're jealous that Mr Wolf likes her more than he likes **YOU.**

Just saying.

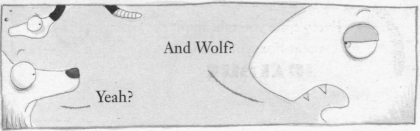

And Wolf?

Yeah?

You told us once that we needed to show the whole world that we're heroes.

You said we just needed to do something that would make the whole world **SIT UP AND NOTICE**.

Well, this is your chance.

Don't blow it, man.

Guys! We're getting close! I can see the . . .

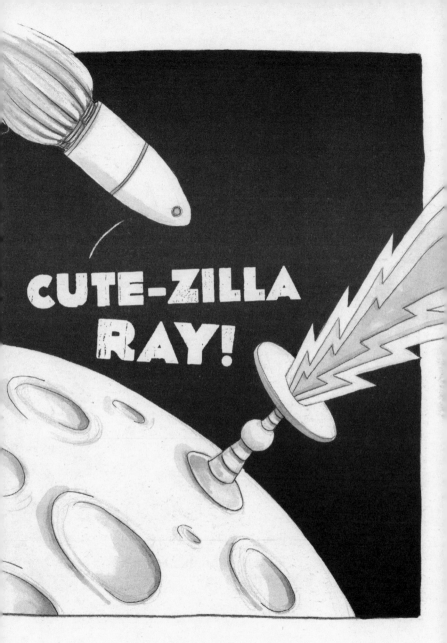

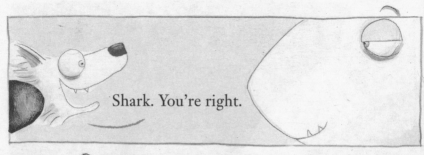

Shark. You're right.

No, he's not!

What?

I'm not jealous!

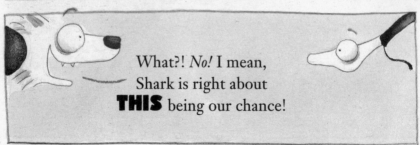

What?! *No!* I mean, Shark is right about **THIS** being our chance!

Oh. Yeah.
Whatever.

This is it, boys!

I'm going down to put on a

SPACESUIT.

It's time to go be a . . .

I'm *not* jealous.

Yeah, yeah. Whatever you say . . .

CHAPTER 4

EVERY SNAKE FOR HIMSELF

OK, fellas. I'm bringing us in to land.

It looks quiet enough out there. But, Wolf? Are you still down in the **LOADING BAY?**

You really should get back up here. Landing might be a little bumpy . . .

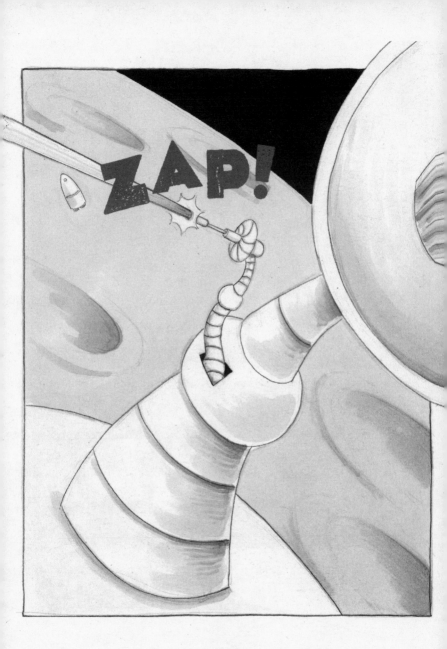

OH, NO!
We're under attack!

Snake! Wait!
Wolf's down there!
You'll trap him!

If we don't seal it . . .
**WE ALL
DIE!**

Something's got us!

We're trapped in some kind of
TRACTOR BEAM!
We're being sucked into the ray!

Helloooo?

On the bright side, at least I have a spacesuit . . .

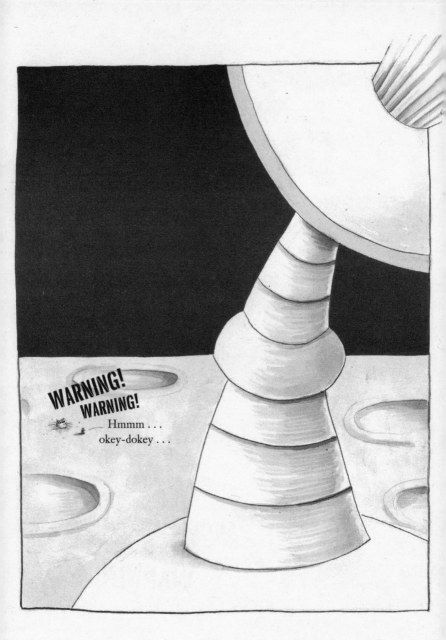

• CHAPTER 5 •
TIED UP...
AGAIN

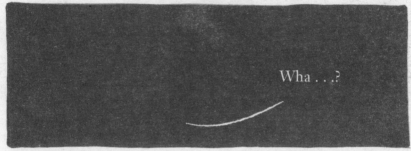

Wha...?

Where...
where am I?

I might be small, Mr Shark.

But I'm **SMARTER** than you.

And **MUCH MORE EVIL.**

How've you been, Mr Shark? Eaten any of your friends today?

That's none of your business, you evil lunatic. The world is ending because of **YOU!**

And . . . Mr Wolf . . . you saw what happened to our lovely Mr Wolf . . .

WELL, YES, the world IS ending because of me.

But don't try to blame ME for Mr Wolf . . .

We all know who's responsible for *that*.

Don't we, Mr Snake?

Leave me alone.

He's right, you little monster! Mr Wolf **IS** your fault. You killed him! You shut that door before he had a chance . . .

YOU'RE LUCKY I CAN'T MOVE!

I can't believe you locked him out. Mr Wolf **BELIEVED IN YOU!** And that's how you repaid him . . .

He's alive? Wolf's alive!

Well, yes and no. You see, he's running out of air. And in precisely eight minutes, he'll stop being a hero ...

PERMANENTLY.

Bring him inside! Please Dr Marmalade! *Please!* Mr Wolf is the best guy we know ...

Oh. Well, if you put it like that, then ...

. . . **NO!**

I think it would be much more fun to watch him run out of air.

Especially since you know it's **ALL YOUR FAULT.**

You monster! If I wasn't tied down I'd—

You'd what?

 You'd *cry* on me? Keep quiet **LEGS** or I'll pull off all your furry little digits and they'll have to start calling you **BODY** instead.

 Hey . . . wait a minute . . .

 Keep quiet, you coward. I don't need your help.

 No, no. Listen to me for a second . . .

Does anyone know where Piranha is?

· CHAPTER 6 ·
OH, NO. ANYTHING BUT THAT . . .

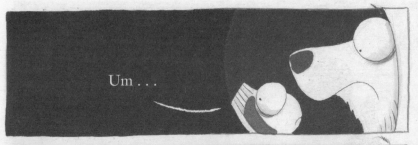

Um . . .

What? What's wrong?
Why are you in my suit?

It's a little embarrassing,
chico . . .

WE HAVE SEVEN
MINUTES OF AIR LEFT–
JUST SPIT IT OUT!

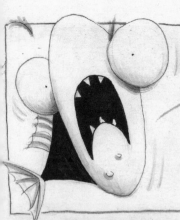

OK!

I ate too many burritos and I needed somewhere to poop!

I'm sorry, can you say that again?

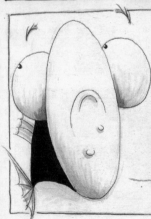

I needed somewhere to poop out my burritos and **I DECIDED TO DO IT IN THE SPACESUIT.**

YOU POOPED IN THIS SPACESUIT?!

NO!

I was **GOING TO** but then you climbed into it! And then I just didn't know what to do next . . .

BUT WHY WERE YOU GOING TO POOP IN A SPACESUIT IN THE FIRST PLACE?!

IT'S A SPACESUIT!

WHO POOPS IN A SPACESUIT?!

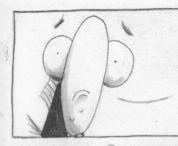

I wasn't sure how to go to the toilet in a spaceship . . .

WHY DIDN'T YOU JUST ASK?!

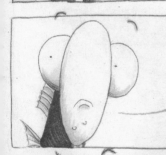

That might have been a better idea . . .

WHAT IS WRONG WITH YOU?!

YOU KNOW WHY WE'RE RUNNING OUT OF AIR? BECAUSE THERE'S A **POOP BURGLAR** IN HERE USING UP HALF OF IT. **THAT'S WHY!**

Wolf. Listen to me. If **ANYONE** can get us out of this mess, it's you.

But you need to *calm down*, hermano.

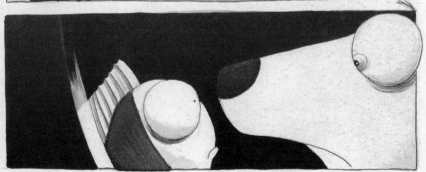

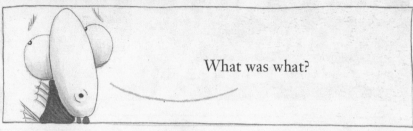

PIRANHA, DID YOU JUST FART IN THE SPACE SUIT?!

Chico. I ate **SO MANY BURRITOS**. That's a **LOT** of beans, you know what I'm saying?

FFAART!

STOP FARTING! IT'S A SPACESUIT— THE SMELL IS TRAPPED IN HERE WITH US! I DON'T WANT TO DIE LIKE THIS!

I'm sorry, hermano! It's the beans!

FFFART!

NOOOOOOOOOO!

• CHAPTER 7 •
IN SPACE, NO-ONE CAN HEAR YOU FART

Oh, no!
Look at his face!
He's run out
of air! He can't
breathe!

Please, Dr Marmalade! Please save him! Look! He's in **AGONY!**

That's weird.
He still has four
minutes of air left.

I wonder what
the problem is?

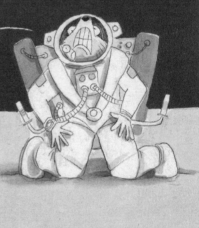

STOP **FARTING, YOU MANIAC!**

I CAN'T BREATHE! MY EYES ARE WATERING . . .

Chico, I'm doing my best but I ate **37 BURRITOS**. There's just not a whole lot I can do to stop it . . .

By being
HEROES,
Mr Piranha!
I think I have
an idea . . .

Great! What is it?

I need you to fart
MORE!

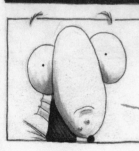

OK, I didn't see that coming . . .

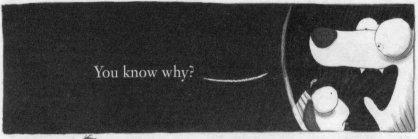

You know why?

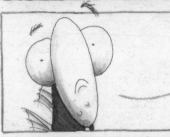

No, I really don't . . .

Because I have a **JET PACK**. And **THAT** is a **BIG, SCARY DEATH-RAY THINGY**. And **YOU** are filling this suit with truly **POISONOUS GAS**.

What does that add up to, Mr Piranha?

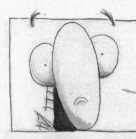

I have no idea . . .

Never mind.
You just keep farting and
I'll find a way to blow up
this machine . . .

No, wait! **I GET IT!**
You think the **FLAMES** from the
JET PACK and the **GAS** from my
FARTS will cause an
EXPLOSION that will destroy
the **CUTE-ZILLA RAY!**

That's right!

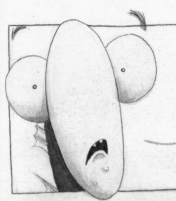

But . . .
There's no way we'll
survive that . . .

No-one
said being
a hero was
going to be
easy, Mr
Piranha.

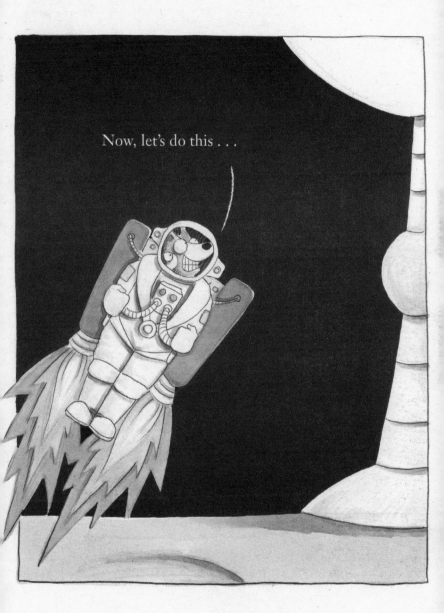

· CHAPTER 8 ·
TIME TO BE A HERO

BACK ON EARTH . . .

Sure, it's cool to be in the **INTERNATIONAL LEAGUE OF HEROES**, but sometimes this job really sucks . . .

Oh, isn't that sweet! He's going
for one last joy-ride before the air
runs out. Isn't he just adorable!?

What is he doing?

I . . . I don't know . . .

I'm sorry, Wolf . . .

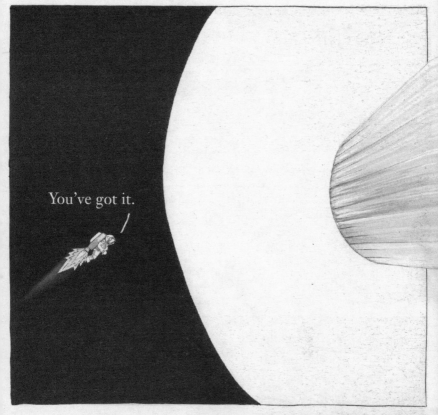

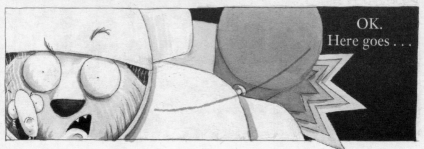

Now let's get in there and
BLOW THIS THING TO BITS!

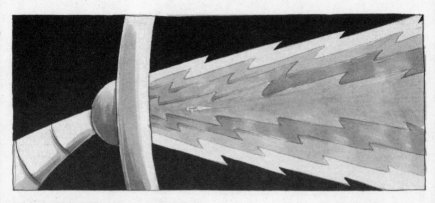

All right!
We're inside it!

I'll fly down
as deep as I
can and . . .

A **WINDOW!**

Just **FART** as much as you can. And I'll head towards those windows down there . . . There's a change of plan, Mr Piranha . . .

Whatever you say, chico . . .

FAAART!

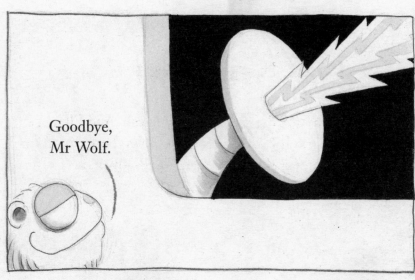

Goodbye,
Mr Wolf.

CRASH!

Wha . . ?

I think you mean

HELLO,

Dr Marmalade!

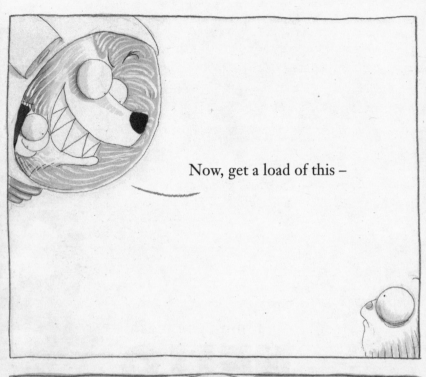

Now, get a load of this –

No, wait! Set me free! I need to do something first . . .

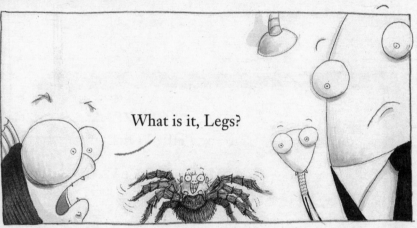

What is it, Legs?

That thing up there is a **CAMERA**. Marmalade sent **US** a message when he turned this thing on. So why don't we send the **WHOLE WORLD** a message before we turn it off?

Are we ready?

Wolfie,
you're on!

Er . . . CITIZENS
of THE WORLD!

My name is Mr Wolf,
and this is my team . . .

. . . the **GOOD GUYS CLUB!**

We really do need a better name, don't we?

First of all, I'd like to apologise for taking a rocket without permission. I feel really bad about that and –

Get on with it, man . . .

Mr Wolf!
You're officially
a HERO!

CHAPTER 9

WHEN IS A GUINEA PIG NOT A GUINEA PIG?

Wolfie!
They're partying
all over the world!

We saved the world!

And everyone **KNOWS** we saved the world!

Things might be a little different now, boys. Looks like we might not be such bad guys after all.

Snake?

Guess what? Shark's right– I *was* jealous.

It made me happy when you thought I could be a good guy, Wolf. It really did.

But then that perfect Agent Fox came along and . . . I just . . . felt like a dirty old snake again.

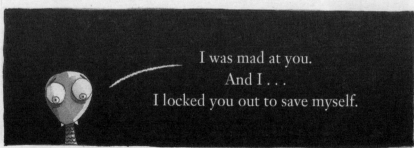

I was mad at you.
And I . . .
I locked you out to save myself.

You know what, Snake? I'm **GLAD** you locked me out.

What?

Because when you locked me out, you **SAVED THE OTHERS**. Sure, that might not exactly have been your reason for doing it. But it's a start. Isn't it?

What's wrong with you, man? I'm no good. Why can't you see that?

I know what I see.
And it's not just
a dirty old snake.
That's for sure.

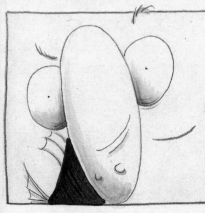

HEY! Sorry to
interrupt your inexplicable
forgiveness of the snake,
but look who's waking up!

No. He's grown **TWO TENTACLES** with **BUTTS** on the ends of them . . .

But that doesn't make any sense . . . guinea pigs don't have tentacles . . .

NO, THEY DON'T. BUT THEN AGAIN, I'M NOT REALLY A GUINEA PIG.

I JUST WEAR A GUINEA PIG SUIT...

OK. Nobody panic.

But there's a *slight* chance that Dr Marmalade might actually be an . . .

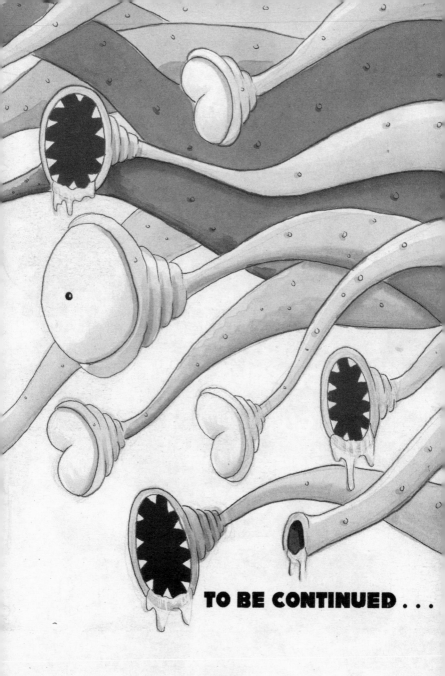

TO BE CONTINUED . . .

GOOD GUYS CLUB SAVES THE WORLD!

There are celebrations across the globe tonight, as the evil **DR RUPERT MARMALADE** has been **DEFEATED!**

TIFFANY FLUFFIT 6

Yes, that's right—every kitten, puppy, bunny, pony and dolphin has been turned from a

FLESH-EATING ZOMBIE

BACK into our cute and furry friends!

And **WHO** do we have to thank?

THE GOOD GUYS CLUB!

AS GOOD AS IT GETS!

Sure, the name might be lame, but I doubt there's a creature on this planet that wouldn't like to give those

CHEEKY, WHOLESOME BOYS

a hug!

The **LOVABLE**
Mr Wolf!

The **BRILLIANT**
Mr Snake!

The **POWERFUL**
Mr Shark!

And
THE OTHER ONE
that is some kind of fish.
Possibly a sardine.

They are the **GREATEST LEGENDS OF OUR TIME!**

ARTIST'S IMPRESSION

And I'd personally like to add that I **ALWAYS** thought they were awesome.

I really did . . .

So let's send them all a great, big . . .

THANK YOU, wherever they may be!

To the gang that saved the world—

NOT BAD, GUYS ..

not bad at all!

It's nice to think of you out there . .

...herever you are . . .

protecting us . . .

you GREAT, BIG, BEAUTIFUL TOUGH GUYS...

· CHAPTER 1 ·
DEEP SPACE, DEEP POO

I think I'm
going to cry . . .

Me too . . .

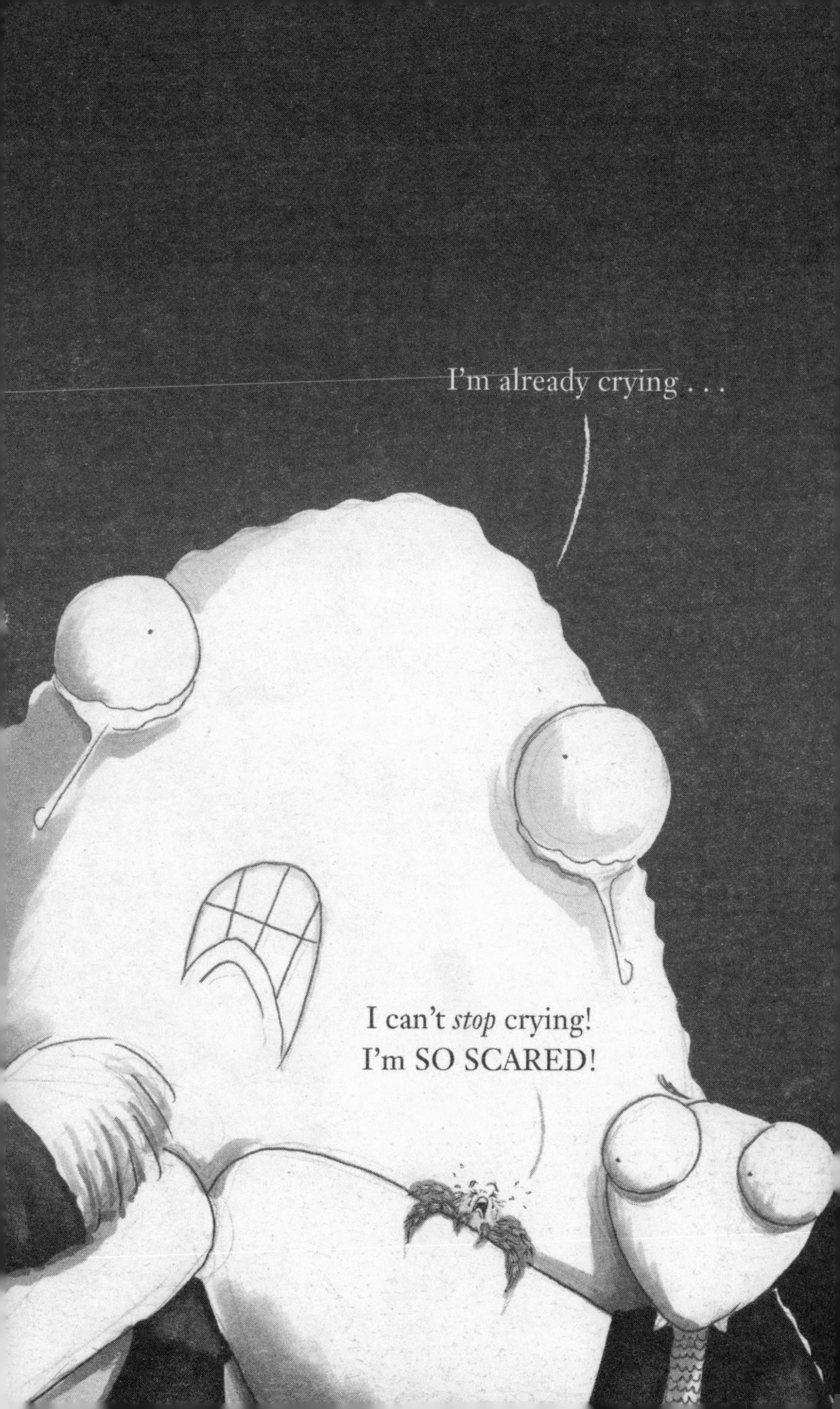
I'm already crying . . .
I can't *stop* crying! I'm SO SCARED!

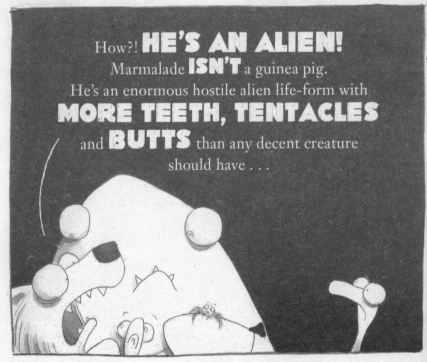

And we're trapped inside its space station on the moon **WITHOUT A ROCKET.**

So **HOW ARE WE GOING TO GET OUT OF HERE?!**

Shhh! It'll hear us! What are we going to do? We can't hide here forever . . .

SPLODGE!

Eeeeee!
Nobody
move . . .

Oh man, this is SO not fair.
We've come so far!
Finally, everyone thinks we're
heroes! We can't die here.
We need a plan . . .

Hey! What's *that*?

Legs!
*Where are
you going?!*

SCUTTLE!

SCUTTLE!

SCUTTLE!

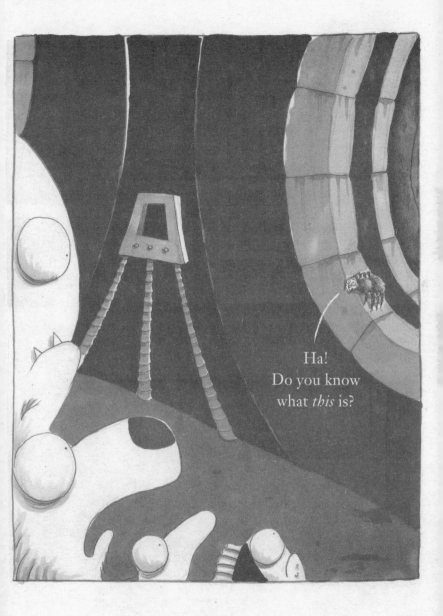

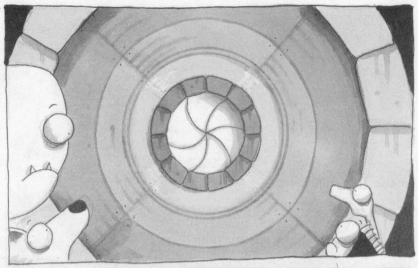

Is it the little room where we all die?

But this is an
ALIEN SPACESHIP!
How will you even know how to work it?

How hard can it be? I bet there
are a whole **BUNCH OF
LANGUAGES** on here and
probably some from **EARTH**
and . . . yep . . . and what if
I just punch in a few
CO-ORDINATES
and . . . yep . . .

ready to launch

destination > earth

I'd say we're
good to go!

Man, you just **HACKED AN ALIEN COMPUTER!** Seriously, we don't give you as much credit as you deserve. Let's hear it for Legs, guys!

OK, I'll tell you what— why don't you stay here and **HAVE A PARADE FOR LEGS** and I'll see you back on Earth. OK?

You are the rudest little—

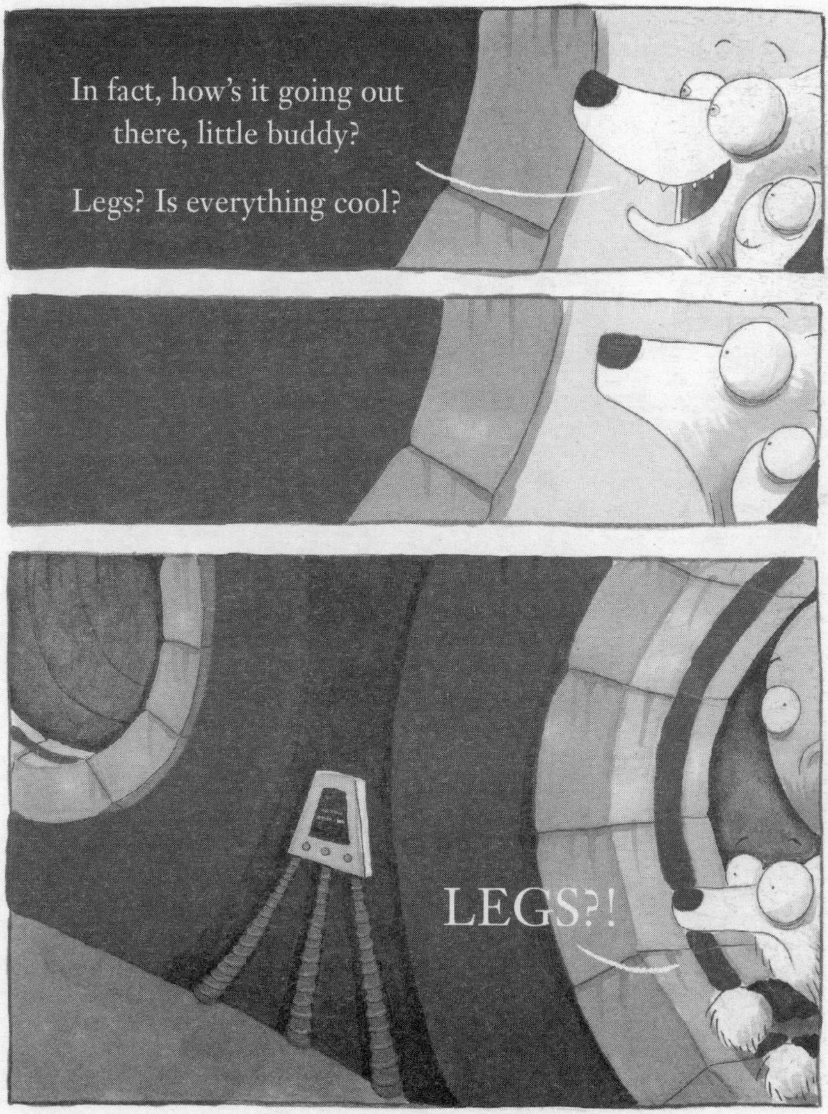
In fact, how's it going out there, little buddy?
Legs? Is everything cool?
LEGS?!

CHAPTER 2

AND THEN THERE WERE FOUR

Are you serious?

YEAH!
I mean, there's **PLENTY** of
these pod things. Legs can just take
the **NEXT ONE**.
He's probably just gone to
GRAB A SANDWICH
or something and I'm sure he
wouldn't mind if we took off and
met him back on—

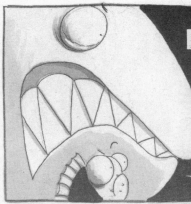

NO-ONE LEAVES UNTIL WE FIND LEGS. **GOT IT?**

I mean, yeah, we **COULD** do that, but don't you think it makes more sense to—

WHAT ARE YOU TALKING ABOUT?!
LEGS IS OUR **FRIEND!**
HE'S THE **ONLY REASON** WE KNOW ABOUT THE ESCAPE PODS IN THE FIRST PLACE AND **YOU WANT TO LEAVE HIM BEHIND?!**

Hey, Piranha! Keep it down!

NO! I'VE HAD IT UP TO HERE WITH THIS ROTTEN LITTLE DIABLO!

I'm just **SAYING**—I think Legs would **WANT** us to save—

YOU ARE THE MOST SELFISH . . .

Piranha!

MEAN-HEARTED . . .

Really, man—*shoosh!*

SON OF A WORM I'VE EVER . . .

Is it just me, or do I have an

ALIEN BUTT

pointed at my face?

Piranha! *Look out!*

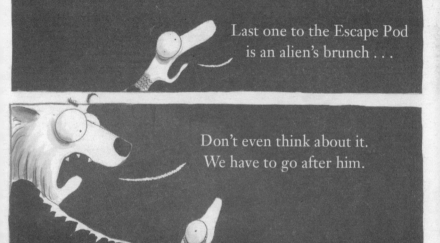

TOOOOOOOOOO MAANNNYYYYYY

He's still ALIVE!
We can follow his voice!

Let's go!

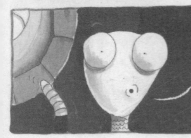

But what about the Escape Pod?
Maybe I should just stay here
and look after it, in case . . .

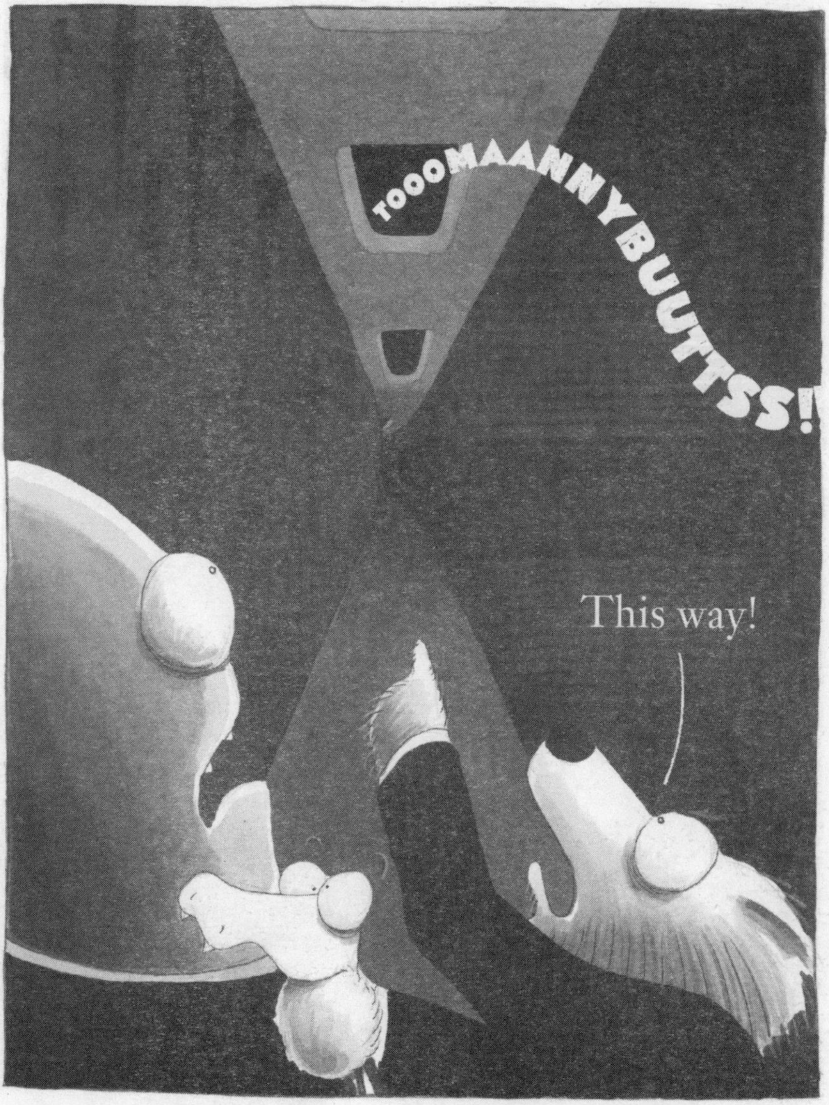
TOOOMAANNYBUUTTSS!!
This way!

· CHAPTER 3 ·
THE LADY ALIEN

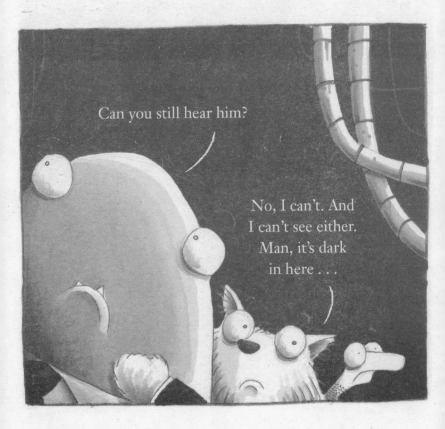

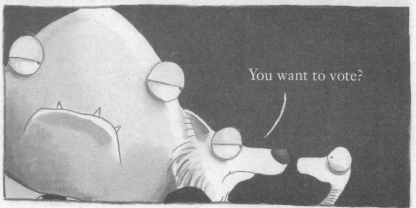

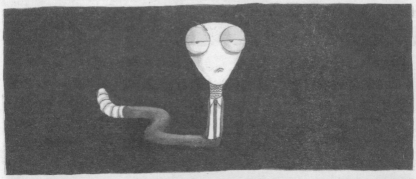

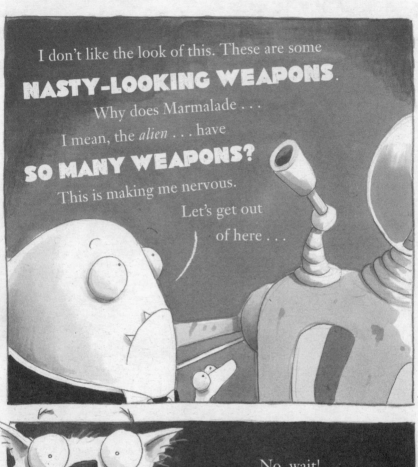

Oh really? And you're trained in using **BIZARRE ALIEN WEAPONS**, are you?

No, but maybe we could figure it out.

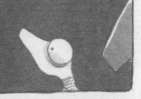

FIGURE IT OUT?!
OK, well why don't you take a few minutes to learn how to

SPEAK ALIEN

and then—have a flick through the

INSTRUCTION MANUALS

and then—mosey on over and TEACH US how to use them too! Yeah. GREAT idea. Let's just all take a seat and

FIGURE IT OUT!

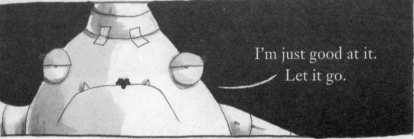

OK, your costumes may have worked in the past, but what you just said is so stupid it makes me want to eat my own face.

Well, I like it.

IT'S INSANE!

C'mon! His costumes *always* work!

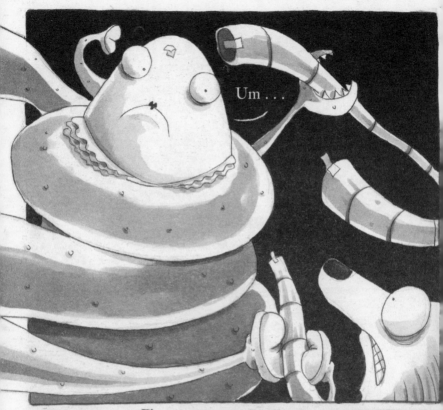

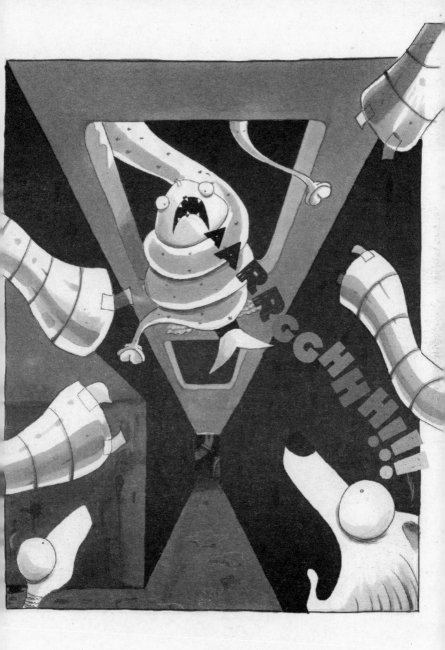

• CHAPTER 4 •
ROUND IN CIRCLES

It's so dark.
Why is it so dark?
It seems to be
getting darker . . .
Don't you think it's
REALLY dark?

YES! WELL SPOTTED! IT'S DARK!
WHAT DO YOU WANT?
A *COOKIE?*
OBVIOUSLY, IT'S DARK.

Give me a break!
I'm **TERRIFIED**!
Everyone's gone. Even Shark!
But we can't give up! If we just
keep searching I **KNOW**
we'll find them. We're getting
CLOSE, I can feel it.

Oh really? We're getting *close*?
Then how do you explain **THIS** . . .

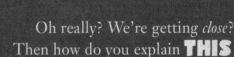

The Escape Pods?!
But that means . . .

It **MEANS** we've been **WALKING AROUND IN CIRCLES**.

Listen to me, Wolf . . .

I'll admit it, **PART OF ME** really does want to be a hero. It's true. Part of me really, *really* does. But you know what I've learnt from following you around on all these stupid missions? Do you know what I've learnt from every ridiculous situation you've put us in?

DO YOU?

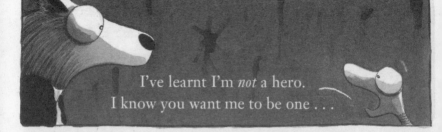

I've learnt I'm *not* a hero.
I know you want me to be one . . .

But I'm really, really not.

I know **YOU** want to be a hero.
And who knows—

MAYBE YOU ARE.

But I also think that you're **CRAZY**.

And I think, one day, you'll make
just one too many stupid decisions
and you **WILL** go and get
yourself eaten by an alien.

And Wolf?

I think that day is today.

I've never had a friend before, Wolf. And even though I do call you an idiot quite a lot . . . I know that you're the best friend I'll ever have. And I don't want to lose you. So . . .

Please get in the Escape Pod with me.

You know I can't, Mr Snake.

And you know why, too.

I can't **MAKE** you do anything, buddy. What you do next is up to you.

There's the **ESCAPE POD**.

If you really want to leave, then go ahead, get in and go. But I have a feeling that you'll do the right—

WHAT?!
I didn't think you'd
actually get in!

Why? Because of my little
speech? Well yeah, I meant it
and everything but there's an

ALIEN WITH
BUTT-HANDS
out there so basically,

ALL BETS ARE OFF
and—

What?

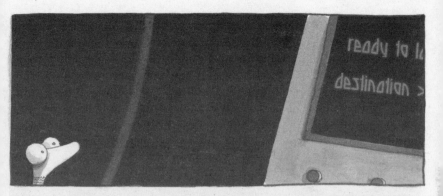

· CHAPTER 5 ·
THE PIT OF DOOM

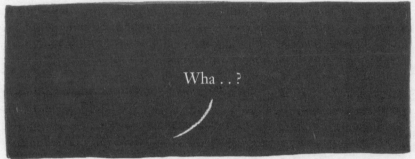

What **IS** this stuff?

I can't say for certain,
but I'm pretty sure it's
DRIED ALIEN SNOT,
hermano.

Piranha!

Hey Wolfie. I've got to be honest—we were kind of hoping next time we saw you, you'd be **RESCUING US**.

It's true. We're pleased to see you, but I think we're all pretty disappointed, too.

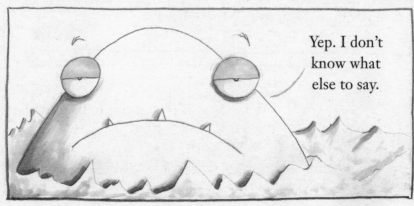

Yep. I don't know what else to say.

No! I believe in him the way I believe in **ALL OF YOU!**

I'm kind of offended by that, hermano.

C'mon guys! I bet he's coming up with a plan to save us **RIGHT NOW!**

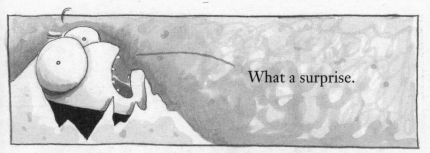

What a surprise.

Yeah. What a shocker.

I can't believe he left us . . .

REALLY?! YOU ACTUALLY **CAN'T** BELIEVE IT?!

· CHAPTER 6 ·

THE END OF THE ROAD

Hey you! Butt-hands!
When you **FART**,
is it from a single tentacle
or do all the disgusting
things go off at once?

WELL, I'M NOT
SURE, LITTLE
FISHY...

226

WELL, NO-ONE TAKES MUCH NOTICE OF SILLY LITTLE GUINEA PIGS. SO I WAS ABLE TO STUDY YOUR PLANET VERY CAREFULLY WITHOUT ANYBODY NOTICING . . .

And what did you learn?

APART FROM THE FACT THAT PIRANHAS AND SHARKS DON'T NEED TO BE IN WATER AS MUCH AS YOU'D THINK?

Yeah. Apart from that . . .

I LEARNT THAT YOUR PLANET IS HELPLESS.

AND IT WILL BE MINE.

I feel so stupid. I thought you were doing all of this just because you didn't like being **CUTE** and **CUDDLY**.

Oh, that wasn't a lie. On my planet, **I AM** cute and cuddly. And **I HATE** it. Don't get me started.

Is your name even 'Marmalade'?

YOU COULDN'T PRONOUNCE MY REAL NAME, WOLF.

Try me.

My name is
KDJFLOERHGCOINWERUHCG
LEIRWFHEKLWJFHXALHW.

Yeah.
Well,
whatevs.

What do you want with us,
KDJFLOERHGCOINWERUHCG
LEIRWFHEKLWJFHXALHW?

WHAT DO I WANT WITH **YOU?** I WANT TO **EAT** YOU. BUT NOT BEFORE I SHOW YOU THE **DESTRUCTION** OF YOUR PLANET!

Yeah, yeah. That sounds great, KDJFdddd—whatever, and yeah, we all saw your weird, creepy **WEAPONS**, but you know what? You don't stand a chance!

OH REALLY? AND WHY'S THAT?

Because there's only **ONE** of you and you're no match for **AGENT FOX** and the **INTERNATIONAL LEAGUE OF HEROES!**

HMMM. THAT FOX IS VERY CLEVER...

BUT, GUESS WHAT?

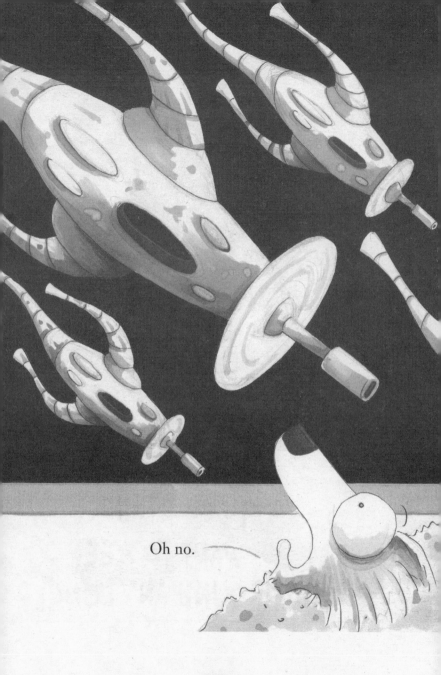

Oh no.

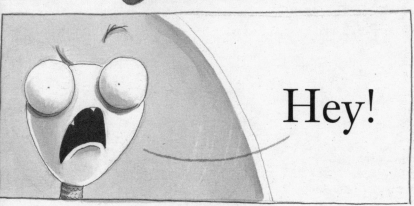

GET AWAY FROM HIM, YOU BUTT-HANDED FREAK!

SNAKE!

· CHAPTER 7 ·
PICK ON SOMEONE YOUR OWN SIZE

CLAMP!

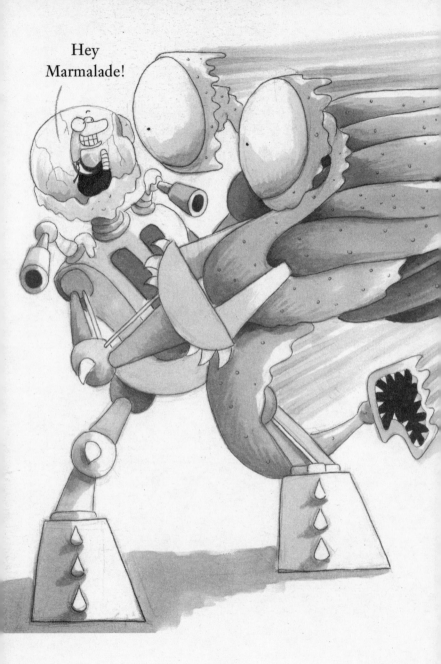

You did it, Snake!

YOU CAME BACK!

YOU CAME BACK!

What changed your mind?

I guess I just finally got sick of being a Bad Guy.

Hey Chicos!
As much as I want to dance my dance of joy right now, there's a whole

ALIEN ARMY OUT THERE WAITING TO DESTROY EARTH!

We need to get home and warn **AGENT FOX.**

It's **KDJFLOER HGCOINWERU HCGLEIRWFHEK LWJFHXALHW!**

But how?!

MY SPECIES CAN HOLD OUR BREATH IN SPACE FOR UP TO NINE WEEKS, IF WE HAVE TO, SO I JUST FLOATED AROUND TO THE BACK DOOR . . .

AND MY **FRIENDS** LET ME **BACK IN.**

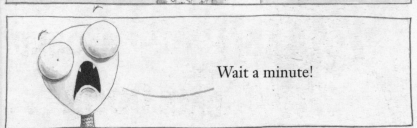

Wait a minute!

Did you just call him **KDJFLOER HGCOINWERU HCGLEIRWFHEK LWJFHXALHW?!**

GET THEM!

• CHAPTER 8 •
THE POD

I'm sorry, Legs, I had to fire off the first Pod to **TRICK** Marmalade. How long will it take you to prep another one?

I'll do it as fast as I can, Mr Hero!

Snake, I'm so proud of you! I mean . . . *how did you get that weapon thing to work?!*

I just . . . figured it out.

SNAP!

EEEEEEE! Oh man, they're everywhere!

Watch out!

SKIID!

Um . . .

Um *WHAT*?!

There's a setting here that kind of bothers me. I'm not sure what it means.

WHO CARES WHAT IT MEANS?!

JUST GET IN HERE AND SEND US BACK TO EARTH!

Yeah . . . OK . . .
I guess it'll be OK . . .

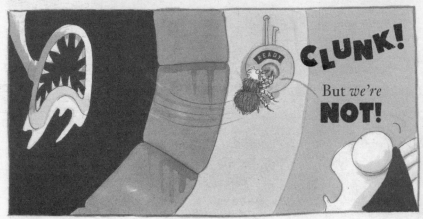

· CHAPTER 9 ·

OUT OF THE FRYING PAN, INTO THE . . .

HANG ON, THAT'S NOT INVENTED YET . . .

I can't lie, Chicos. I thought there'd be a bit of a crowd waiting to welcome us. I've got my Party Pants on . . .

Yeah. And we have to warn Agent Fox.

Where is everyone?

Maybe we're just in the **WRONG SPOT.**

Did we land in another country or something?

Ahhhh, no. As far as I can tell, we've landed right back where we arranged to **MEET AGENT FOX.**

What do you mean, Legs? We're in the **MIDDLE OF NOWHERE**. You must be reading that thing wrong.

Hmmm. I wish I was . . .

Don't stress, guys! We're home! That's the main thing. We're home, but this time it's *different*. This time we're **HEROES!**

Ohhhhh. Being heroes isn't the only thing that's different . . .

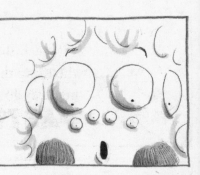

What do you mean, Legs?

Well, remember that setting that was bothering me? It seems . . . it was the control for a slightly

DIFFERENT KIND OF TRAVEL . . .

You mean that's the thing that made us go so **FAST?**

Well, maybe . . . but that's not what I mean . . .

Spit it out, Spider!
WHERE ARE WE?!

Mr Snake, the question isn't **'WHERE'** . . .

65 MILLION BC?! Are you kidding?! **65 MILLION BC?!** But that's when . . .

When what?

Oh my stars! You're right! That's when there were . . .

That's when there were

WHAT?!

DINOS

TO BE CONTINUED . . .

IT'S ON.

EPISODE 7

COMING SOON!